WORKBOOKS

2nd Grade

Science

Author Hugh Westrup

Educational Consultant Kara Pranikoff

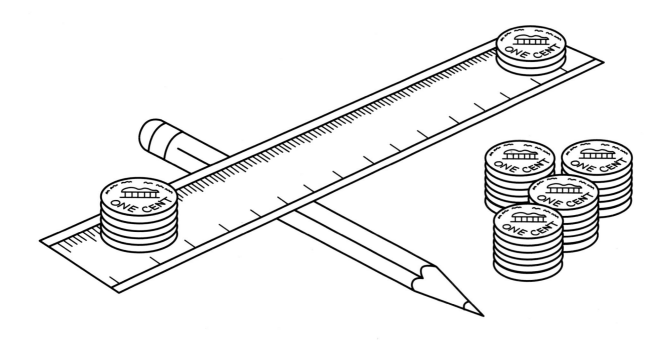

LONDON, NEW YORK, MUNICH,
MELBOURNE, and DELHI

US Editor Nancy Ellwood
US Educational Consultant Kara Pranikoff
Senior Editors Fran Baines, Cécile Landau
Managing Art Editor Richard Czapnik
Art Director Martin Wilson
Pre-production Francesca Wardell

DK Delhi
Asst. Editor Nishtha Kapil
Asst. Art Editors Tanvi Nathyal, Yamini Panwar
DTP Designer Anita Yadav
Dy. Managing Editor Soma B. Chowdhury

First American Edition, 2014
Published in the United States by DK Publishing
4th floor, 345 Hudson Street, New York, New York 10014

14 15 16 17 10 9 8 7 6 5 4 3 2 1
001—197332—01/14

Copyright © 2014 Dorling Kindersley Limited

A catalog record for this book
is available from the Library of Congress
ISBN: 978-1-4654-1729-9

DK books are available at special discounts when purchased in bulk
for sales promotions, premiums, fund-raising, or educational use.
For details, contact:
DK Publishing Special Markets
4th floor, 345 Hudson Street, New York, New York 10014
SpecialSales@dk.com.

Printed and bound in China by Leo Paper Products Ltd.

All images © Dorling Kindersley Limited
For further information see: www.dkimages.com
Discover more at
www.dk.com

Contents

This chart lists all the topics in the book. Once you have completed each page, stick a star in the correct box below.

Page	Topic	Star
4	Scientists	☆
5	Flowers	☆
6	Pollination	☆
7	Pollinators	☆
8	Conifers	☆
9	Carnivorous Plants	☆
10	Insects	☆
11	Social Insects	☆
12	Types of Insect	☆
13	Arachnids	☆

Scientists study different parts of Earth and nature.

Label the name of each scientist to complete the sentences.

| Botanist | Chemist | Zoologist |

A person who studies chemical reactions is a _Chemis___.

A person who studies plants is a _Botanist_.

A person who studies animals is a _Zoologist_

Which objects interest each scientist? Write **B** next to the objects that interest a botanist, **C** next to the ones that interest a chemist, and **Z** next to the ones that interest a zoologist.

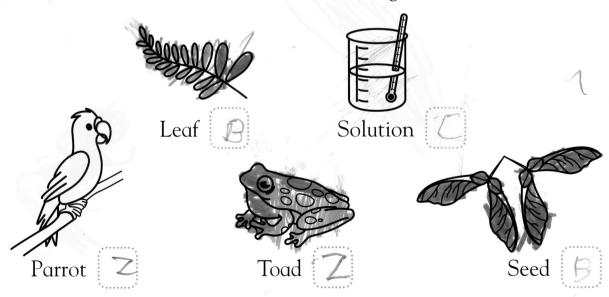

Leaf _B_

Solution _C_

Parrot _Z_

Toad _Z_

Seed _B_

Flowers contain the male and female parts of a plant. The male cells are a powder called pollen, and are produced in the stamen. Visiting animals, attracted by the colorful petals and scent of the flower, pick up the pollen from one flower and deposit it on another. The female part of a flower is called the pistil. When the pistil is dusted by the pollen of another flower, it is called pollination. When pollen moves down the pistil, seeds form. The seeds grow into new plants.

Use the words in the box to complete the sentences.

| Petals | Pistil | Pollen | Seed | Stamen |

Petals

Seed

Stamen

Pistil

1. The **STamen** is the male part of the flower where pollen is made.

2. The **Pistil** is the female part of the flower where seeds are held.

3. _____ is a powder made by the male part of a plant.

4. _____ are the colorful parts of a flower that attract animals.

5. A _____ grows into a new plant.

FACTS

Pollination is the transfer of pollen from one plant to another. Many flowering plants depend on honeybees to pollinate them.

These pictures show the steps a honeybee takes to pollinate a flower. Match each step with the sentence that describes what is happening in the picture.

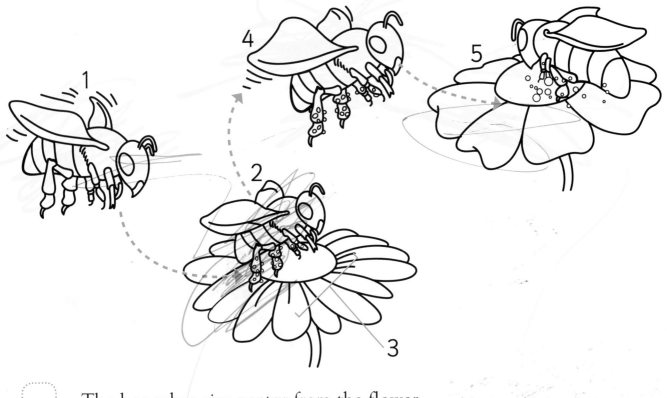

◯   The honeybee sips nectar from the flower.

◯   The honeybee is attracted to the scent and color of a flower.

◯   The honeybee is attracted to a new flower. As it sips nectar from the new flower, pollen falls off its legs onto the pistil.

◯   Pollen sticks to the honeybee's body.

◯   The honeybee flies away from the flower with pollen stuck to its legs.

FACTS

Flowering plants depend on wind, water, and animals to pollinate them. Many different types of animals pass pollen from flower to flower as they feed.

Draw a line between the animal and the sentence that describes how it pollinates flowers.

Butterfly

Lizard

Bat

Hummingbird

The fur of this animal gets covered in pollen as it feeds from plants that flower at night.

This animal has a long thin beak to reach into flowers and drink the nectar. The pollen rubs onto its feathers.

This animal has a long tongue, called a proboscis, that acts like a drinking straw. Pollen sticks to its legs as it feeds.

The bodies of these small reptiles get covered in pollen as they climb right inside flower heads to eat the sweet nectar.

A conifer is a tree that produces its seeds in cones. Most coniferous trees are evergreen—they keep their leaves all year long. Some also have long, thin leaves called needles.

Circle the tree branches that belong to conifers.

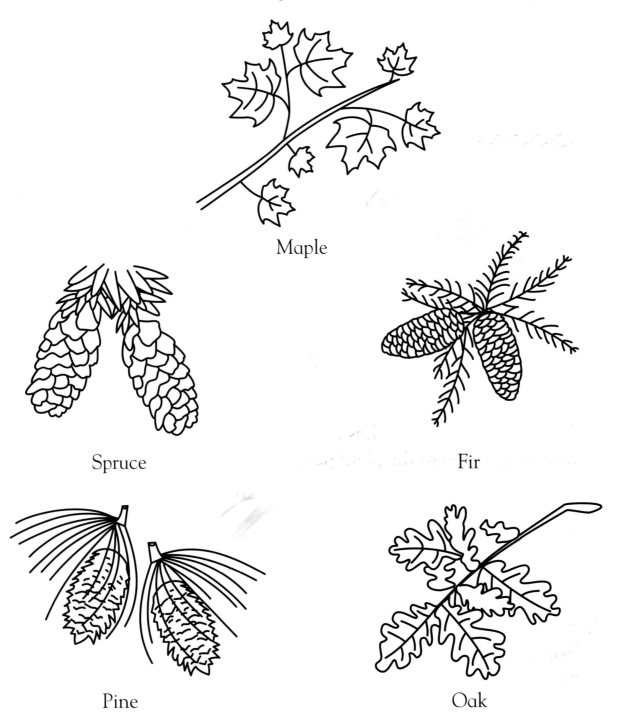

Maple

Spruce

Fir

Pine

Oak

Some plants are carnivorous. They trap and eat small animals, mostly insects.

Look at these three pictures of carnivorous plants, then read the descriptions below and complete the sentences.

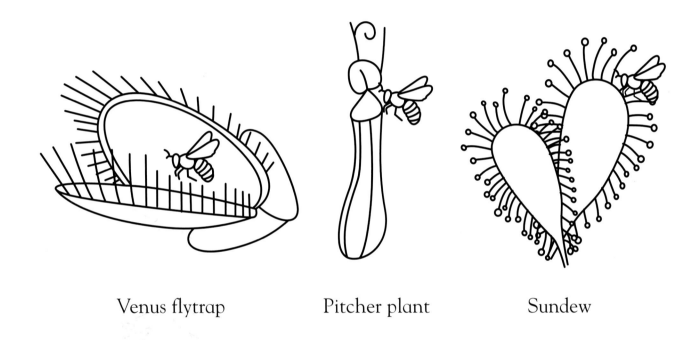

Venus flytrap   Pitcher plant   Sundew

1. A .... has tentacles covered with a sweet, sticky goo. Insects attracted to the plant get stuck in the goo and are eaten.

2. A .... has a deep cup full of a sweet nectar that lures insects into it. Hairs inside the cup keep the insects from getting out.

3. A .... has leaves at the end of each stalk that open like a clamshell. When an insect lands on the leaves to drink the nectar, the leaves snap shut and trap the insect inside.

All insects have a body divided into three parts: the head, the thorax, where the legs and wings are attached, and the abdomen, which holds most of the animal's organs. Insects have six legs.

An ant is a common insect. Use the words in the box to label the parts of the ant.

| Abdomen | Antenna | Head | Leg | Thorax |

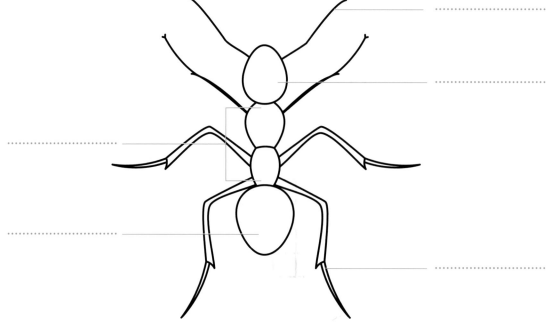

Circle the insects.

Termite   Worm   Mosquito   Crab

FACTS

Insects that live in a group are called social insects. Honeybees live together in a hive. Each type of bee has a special job. The queen bee lays all the eggs. The worker bees are females who gather food to feed the young bees. Drones are male bees who mate with the queen.

Use the words in the box to complete the crossword.

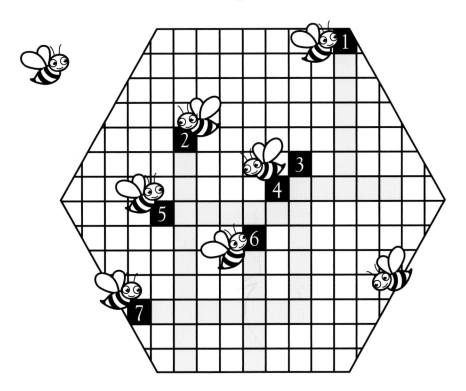

Dance	Drones	Honeycomb	Nectar
Pollen	Queen	Workers	

Across:

4. What honeybees do to tell one another where to find flowers.

5. A sweet fluid that honeybees collect from flowers.

7. The adult females that feed the young in a hive.

Down:

1. A powdery substance that honeybees carry from flower to flower.

2. The six-sided cells that honeybees build in their hive.

3. The male adults in a hive.

6. The bee that lays all of the eggs.

Scientists have found more than 900,000 types of insect.

Use the words in the box to name the insects.

| Beetle | Cockroach | Dragonfly | Flea | Fly |
| Grasshopper | | Ladybug | Wasp | |

Arachnids are animals that have two main body parts, and four pairs of legs. Arachnids include spiders, scorpions, ticks, and mites.

Study these pictures of four arachnids. Complete the chart that describes the ways in which arachnids look different from insects.

Spider

Tick

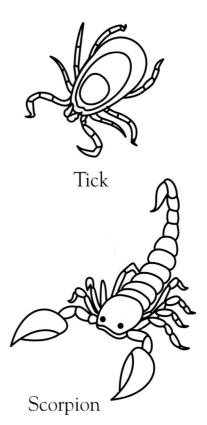

Mite

Scorpion

	Arachnid	**Insect**
How many legs?		
How many body segments?		
Does it have wings?		

FACTS

A butterfly is an insect that looks very different at each stage of its life. This change is called metamorphosis.

Use the words in the box to label each stage in the life of a butterfly and complete the sentences below.

| Adult | Caterpillar | Chrysalis | Egg |

....

....

1. The .... is a tiny round or oval object. It is often attached to a leaf or a stem of a plant.

2. The .... is long and wormlike. It eats and eats to grow quickly.

3. The .... is a case that protects the caterpillar as it rests while its body changes.

4. The .... emerges with colorful wings and flies away.

Life Cycle of a Grasshopper

A grasshopper is an example of an insect that has the same body shape throughout most of its life.

Use the words to label each stage in the life of a grasshopper and complete the sentences below.

| Adult | Nymph | Egg |

....

....

1. A grasshopper starts as a tiny ...., usually attached to a leaf or stem.

2. A baby grasshopper is called a ....

3. A fully grown .... grasshopper has large legs for hopping.

★ Life Cycle of a Frog

A frog is an amphibian—it spends part of its life in water, and part on land. Frogs are very different at each stage of their life cycle. This change is called metamorphosis.

Use the words to label the stages in the life of a frog.

Eggs	Frog	Froglet	Tadpole	Tadpole with legs

All animals change as they mature into adulthood.

Draw lines between the young animals and the adult animals they will become.

Young Animals

Adult Animals

Chick

Dog

Caterpillar

Toad

Tadpole

Fly

Puppy

Chicken

Maggot

Moth

A trait is a distinguishing characteristic—the way something looks or behaves. Scientists study traits to understand how living things are related.

Write your name at the top of the second column and the names of two members of your family at the top of the other columns. Record the age, height, and other traits about you and your family members.

Traits	Relative	Your Name	Relative
Age			
Male or Female			
Height			
Eye color			
Hair color			
Shoe size			

Compare the information.

What traits do you share with your relatives?

....

....

What traits are different?

....

....

An adaptation is a feature that helps living things to survive in the habitat they live in.

Read the sentences and match them to the correct animal by putting the number in the box. We have done the first one for you.

1. This animal's keen sense of hearing helps it detect prey at night.

2. This strong animal catches its prey with its sharp claws and strong jaws.

3. This animal uses its long tail to help it climb trees and cling to branches.

4. This animal has teeth strong enough to cut down trees to build dams.

5. This animal has a beak with a pouch so it can scoop up fish from the water.

6. This animal has a long neck so it can eat leaves high up in the trees.

 4

An endangered species is a plant or an animal that is in danger of becoming extinct, or dying out forever.

Use the words to name the endangered animals pictured below.

| African wild dog | Chimpanzee | Giant Panda | Orangutan |
| Rhinoceros | | Tiger | |

....

....

....

The digestive system turns food into nutrients that our bodies need to survive.

Use the words in the box to complete the sentences.

Esophagus	Large Intestine	Mouth	Small Intestine	Stomach

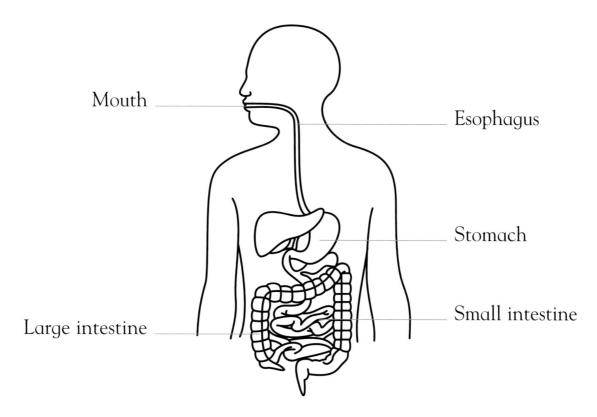

1. The digestion process begins in the ...., where food is chewed and mixed with saliva.

2. The .... connects the mouth to the stomach.

3. The .... contains an acid fluid that breaks down food.

4. The .... is a long tube where nutrients from digested food pass into the bloodstream.

5. The .... mixes water with food that you can't digest and turns it into waste.

The cells of the body are supplied with the oxygen they need by the respiratory system. Air containing oxygen is breathed into the body and enters the bloodstream through the lungs. Carbon dioxide is breathed out as waste.

Use the words to label the parts of the respiratory system and to complete the sentences.

Lungs	Nose	Trachea

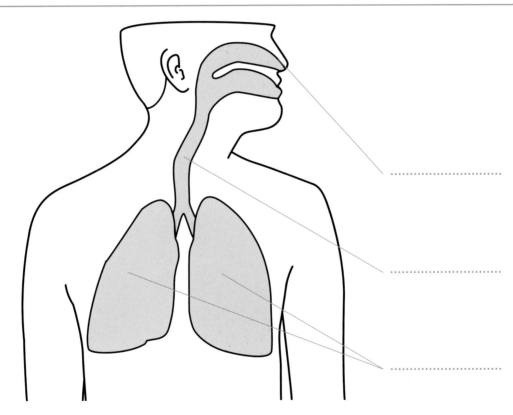

1. Air is inhaled and exhaled through the ....

2. The .... is also called the windpipe, and it directs air into the lungs.

3. The .... are large organs that expand like balloons as they fill with air, and contract as air is squeezed out. Here, oxygen passes into the bloodstream, and carbon dioxide is removed.

The nervous system is made up of the brain, the spinal cord, and nerves. The brain controls the body by sending signals down the spinal cord. The spinal cord sends the signals back and forth between the brain and nerves all over the body.

Use the words to label the picture and to complete the sentences that explain the parts of the nervous system.

Brain	Spinal cord	Nerves

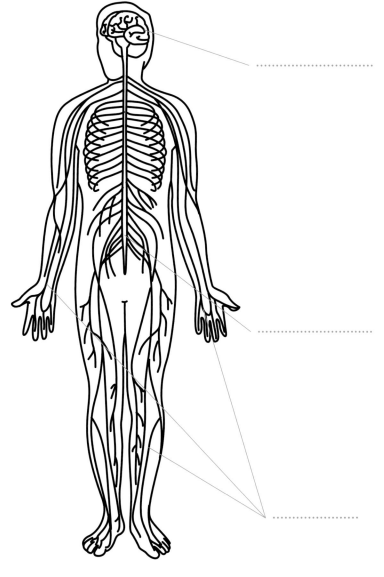

1. The .... is the control center of the nervous system. It enables us to think, feel, and remember, and it instructs the body to move.

2. The .... relays nerve signals between the brain and the body.

3. A network of .... sends and receives information about what is going on in and around the body.

★ Friction

FACTS

The resistance that occurs where surfaces rub together is a force called friction. Rough surfaces create more friction. Smooth surfaces create less friction.

TEST **What You Need:**

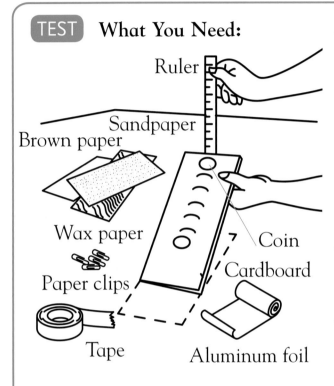

Ruler
Sandpaper
Brown paper
Wax paper
Paper clips
Tape
Coin
Cardboard
Aluminum foil

What To Do:

1. Place the cardboard on a flat surface. Hold the ruler upright against one of the narrow ends of the cardboard. Place a coin on the cardboard at this end.

2. Pressed against the ruler, slowly lift the end of the cardboard.

3. When the coin slides down the cardboard, record the height of the cardboard.

4. One at a time, attach each of the other coverings to the cardboard. Repeat the test.

RESULT Predict the height at which the coin will slide on each covering. Record the results.

Covering	Prediction	Height of Lift
Cardboard		
Brown paper		
Wax paper		
Sandpaper		
Aluminum foil		

How does the covering change the friction?

....

....

Friction helps people play sports. In some sports, you need high friction to help grip smooth surfaces. In other sports, you need low friction so that things slide over surfaces smoothly.

The arrows point to places where friction is important in each sport. Check (✔) whether there is high friction or low friction at this point. Then explain how that amount of friction helps people play each sport.

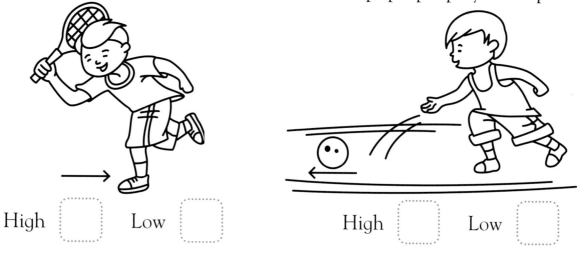

High ☐   Low ☐

High ☐   Low ☐

....

....

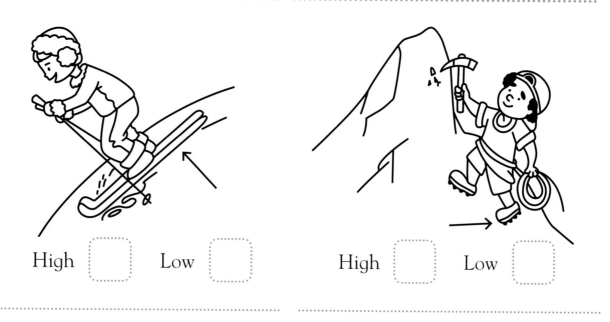

High ☐   Low ☐

High ☐   Low ☐

....

....

Simple machines make work easier for us. They allow us to push or pull things over greater distances.

Use the words in the box to complete the definitions of six simple machines, then draw a line between each sentence and the machine it describes.

Inclined plane	Lever	Pulley	Screw	Wedge	Wheel

1. A .... is a circular device that turns around an axle.

2. A .... is a stiff bar that turns on a fulcrum, or pivot.

3. A .... is an object with at least one slanting side that ends in a sharp edge.

4. An .... is a sloping surface that connects a lower level to a higher level.

5. A .... is a grooved wheel and a rope or chain.

6. A .... is a shaft with a groove that spirals around it.

Simple machines can help us do many jobs.

Circle the six simple machines that are being used in this picture.

★ Levers

FACTS

The point at which a lever turns is called a fulcrum. The fulcrum needs to be in the right place for the lever to work properly.

TEST

What You Need:

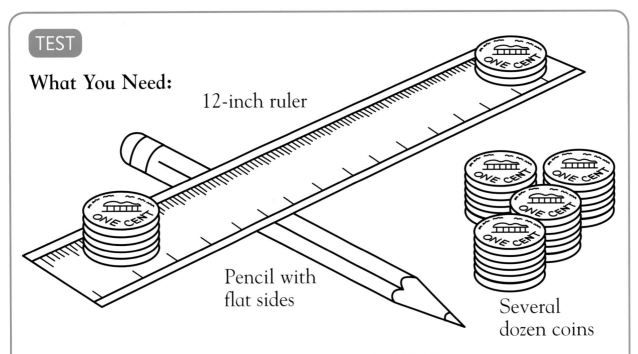

12-inch ruler

Pencil with flat sides

Several dozen coins

What To Do:

1. Set up the test as shown above. The ruler is the lever.

2. Slide the pencil under the ruler at the 4-inch mark. This is the lever's fulcrum, or pivot.

3. Stack 5 pennies between the end of the ruler and the 1-inch mark.

4. At the other end of the ruler, stack pennies one at a time until the end with the 5 pennies rises off the table.

5. Place the pencil at different points under the ruler and repeat the test. Record the results.

RESULT

Record the number of pennies it takes to lift the 5 coins with the fulcrum at different points.

Position of Pencil Under Ruler	Number of Coins
3 inches	
4 inches	
5 inches	
6 inches	

Matter is the name used to describe all the different material that makes up the universe. The amount of matter in an object is known as its mass. Matter also takes up space, which is known as its volume. There are three states of matter: solid, liquid, and gas. A solid keeps its shape. A liquid flows, and takes the shape of the container it is in. A gas expands to fill its container.

Use the words in the box to complete the sentences about matter.

Gas	Liquid	Mass	Solid	States	Volume

The Three States of Matter

Solid

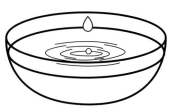

Liquid

Gas

1. Matter occurs in three _____.

2. A _____ is matter that has a shape of its own.

3. A _____ is matter that flows and takes the shape of the container it is in.

4. A _____ is matter that expands to fill any container it is put into.

5. The amount of matter in an object is called its _____.

6. The amount of space occupied by matter is called _____.

FACTS

Some foods change when they get hot or cold.

Look at these questions about what happens to foods when the temperature changes. Put a check (✔) next to the correct answer.

1. What happens to chocolate on a warm day?

It gets softer.

It gets harder.

2. What happens to bread when you toast it?

It gets softer.

It gets harder.

3. What happens to butter when it is left in the fridge?

It gets softer.

It gets harder.

4. What happens to a popsicle when it is out of the freezer?

It gets softer.

It gets harder.

5. What happens when you fry an egg?

It gets softer.

It gets harder.

A solution is a mixture in which the different substances mix together so well that they seem like a single substance.

Put a check (✓) next to the substances that make a solution when added to water.

Salt ☐

Pepper ☐

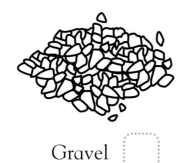

Gravel ☐

Flour ☐

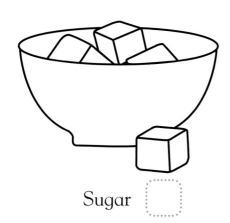

Sugar ☐

Sand ☐

Sounds can be made in many different ways.

Use the words in the box to describe correctly how these musical instruments are played to make sounds.

Beating	Blowing	Plucking	Scraping	Shaking

Guitar

Recorder

Maracas

Violin

Drum

1. The violin is played by .... the bow across the strings.

2. .... into a recorder makes a sweet sound.

3. Maracas are played by ....

4. .... the surface of the drum makes a booming noise.

5. The guitar is played by either strumming or .... the strings.

You can make a sound by blowing over the neck of a bottle. The sound will change if you pour water into the bottle.

TEST **What You Need:**

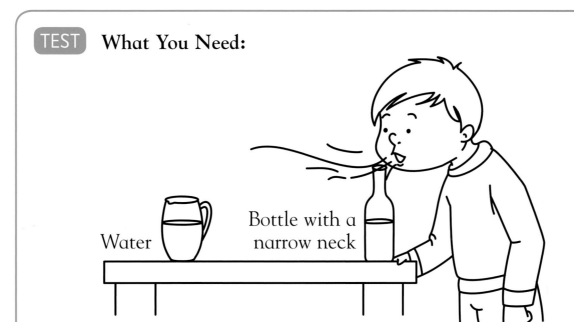

Water

Bottle with a narrow neck

What To Do:

1. Take the empty bottle, with the lid off, and place it on a table. Practice blowing over the neck until you can hear a hollow sound. Remember what the noise sounds like.

2. Pour some water into the bottle and blow again. Listen carefully to the sound again.

3. Add more water, a little at a time, and blow again. Note if the sound is changing.

RESULT

What happened to the sound when you added more and more water?

....

....

★ Water

Water changes state when it freezes.

TEST **What You Need:**

Freezer

Kitchen scale

Pen and paper

Magic marker

Plastic cup of water

What To Do:

1. Weigh the cup with water on the scale. Record the weight.

2. Use the magic marker to mark the level of the water on the cup. The mark is a measure of the volume of water. It tells you how much space the water occupies in the cup.

3. Put the cup in a freezer. Remove the cup several hours later and weigh.

4. Mark the level of the water surface with the pen.

RESULT

Weight before: .... Weight after: ....

Answer these questions about how the cup has changed:
A. Has the state of water changed from a liquid to something else?

....

B. Has the water undergone a change in weight?

....

C. Is the level of water in the cup different to the level of ice?

....

Evaporation

Evaporation is the change of a liquid into a gas. This usually happens because of an increase in temperature.

TEST **What You Need:**

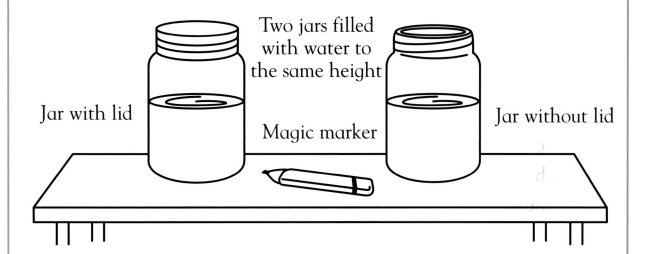

Two jars filled with water to the same height

Jar with lid

Magic marker

Jar without lid

What To Do:

1. With a marker, mark each jar at the level of the water. Put a lid on one jar.

2. Put the jars on a shelf.

RESULT

After two days, observe any changes to the water in each jar. What happened in the jar with the lid? What happened to the jar without the lid? Why?

....

....

....

....

FACTS

Condensation is the process in which a gas turns into liquid. This usually happens because of a drop in temperature.

TEST

What You Need:

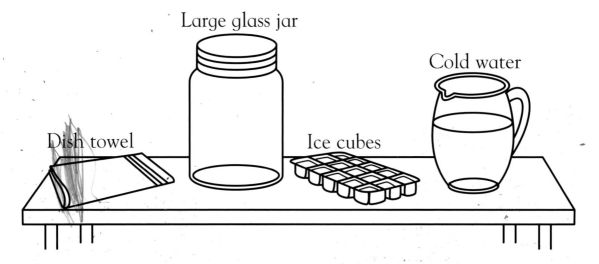

Large glass jar

Cold water

Dish towel

Ice cubes

What To Do:

1. Dry any moisture off the jar with the dish towel.

2. Fill the jar with ice cubes and cold water.

3. After an hour observe the jar.

RESULT

Has the outside of the jar changed in any way?
Explain what happened.

....

....

....

Water is constantly evaporating into the air, condensing as it rises and cools, and falling back to Earth as rain. This movement occurs in a circular pattern, called the water cycle.

Add arrows to this diagram to show the direction of the water cycle and then complete the sentences below.

| Clouds | Condenses | Evaporates | Water Cycle |

1. As the sun heats water in the seas and rivers, the water .... The water turns into water vapor—a gas.

2. When the water vapor rises into the sky and meets cold air it forms ....

3. When the cloud rises high in the sky where the air is cooler, the water vapor .... to form water droplets, or rain.

4. Rain falls to the ground and forms rivers that flow back to the sea, and the .... begins again.

Measuring Rainfall

FACTS

You can measure the amount of rain that falls over a period of time in a rain gauge.

TEST **What You Need:**

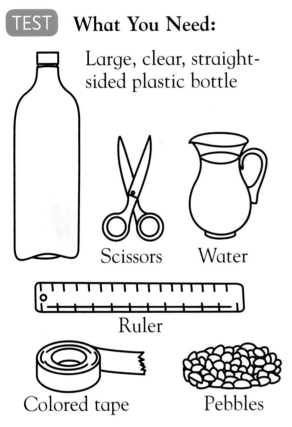

Large, clear, straight-sided plastic bottle

Scissors   Water

Ruler

Colored tape   Pebbles

 What To Do:

1. Ask an adult to help you cut the bottle in two, about two-thirds up the bottle. Try to make a straight cut.

2. Put the pebbles in the bottom half of the bottle. Stick some tape to the side of the bottle, just above the pebbles. Add water until it reaches the top of the tape.

3. Turn the top part of the bottle upside down, and place it in the bottom half of the bottle (as shown below).

4. Put outside in a place where it is open to the sky.

RESULT

After a rainfall, use the ruler to measure the amount of water above the tape. Then pour water out until it is level with the top of the tape again. Keep a record of the amount of rainfall each week during the year and see how it changes from season to season.

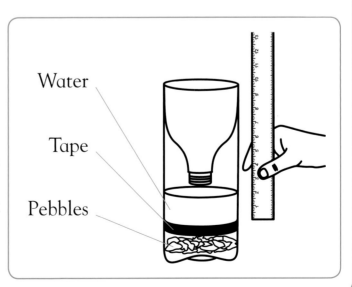

Water

Tape

Pebbles

Weather changes from day to day.

Record the weather conditions each day for a week in the chart below. The words in the box below may help you.

| Calm | Cloudy | Rainy | Snowy | Sunny | Windy |

Day	Weather
Monday	
Tuesday	
Wednesday	
Thursday	
Friday	
Saturday	
Sunday	

★ Air Temperature

The world's weather is caused by heat from the sun. The power of the sun affects the air temperature, which varies from day to day.

The line graph below shows the average temperature each day during a week in January. Use the graph to answer these questions.

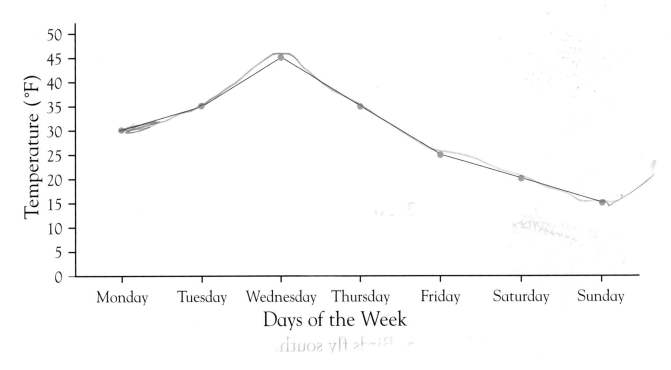

1. Which day was the coldest? ....

2. What day was the warmest? ....

3. What was the temperature on Tuesday? ....

4. What was the temperature on Friday? ....

5. On which two days was the temperature the same? ....

6. On what day was the temperature 10 degrees colder than it was on Monday? ....

7. How many degrees warmer was it on Wednesday than Tuesday? ....

As the seasons change, the temperature and the amount of daylight change. This affects plant growth and the behavior of many animals.

Each sentence describes an event that happens during one of the four seasons. Write **Sp** for spring, **Su** for summer, **F** for fall, or **W** for winter in the boxes.

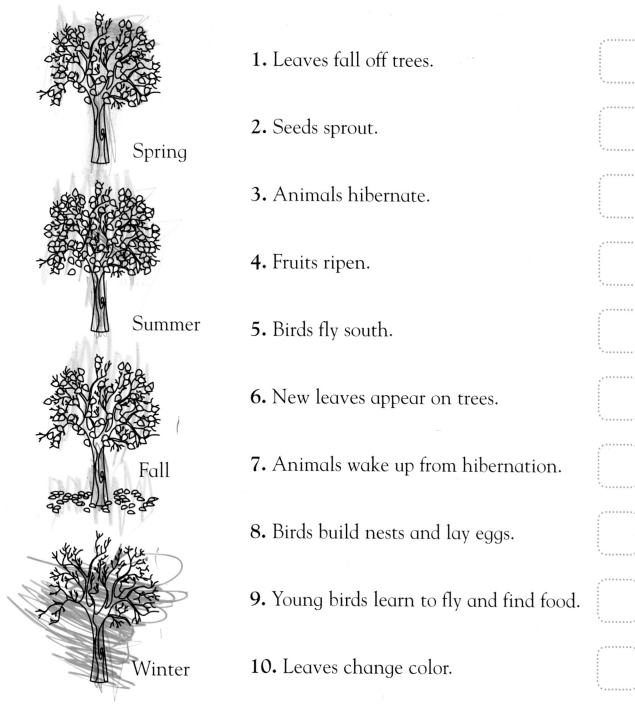

Spring

Summer

Fall

Winter

1. Leaves fall off trees.

2. Seeds sprout.

3. Animals hibernate.

4. Fruits ripen.

5. Birds fly south.

6. New leaves appear on trees.

7. Animals wake up from hibernation.

8. Birds build nests and lay eggs.

9. Young birds learn to fly and find food.

10. Leaves change color.

FACTS

Some things you can squash and bend, stretch and twist, and when you let go, they return to their original shape.

Look at each object and put a check (✔) in the box if it bends, squashes, stretches, and/or returns to its shape.

	Bends	Squashes	Stretches	Returns to its shape
Paper ball	☐	☐	☐	☐
Sponge	☐	☐	☐	☐
Rubber band	☐	☐	☐	☐
Tomato	☐	☐	☐	☐
Plastic ruler	☐	☐	☐	☐
Rubber ball	☐	☐	☐	☐

If you can see through a material when you hold it up to your eyes, it is called a transparent material. Some materials you cannot see through at all. Others are not transparent, but if you shine a flashlight on them, you can see the glow of the light on the other side.

TEST **What You Need:**

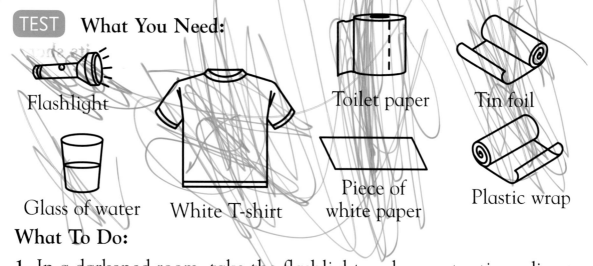

Flashlight

Glass of water White T-shirt

Toilet paper

Piece of white paper

Tin foil

Plastic wrap

What To Do:

1. In a darkened room, take the flashlight and, one at a time, direct the beam at each of the different materials.

2. Observe how much light passes through each of the materials to come out the other side.

RESULT

Put a check (✓) in the correct box and record your results.

Materials	Transparent	Not Transparent	Can See Flashlight Glow
Glass of water			
White T-shirt			
White paper			
Plastic wrap			
Toilet paper			
Tin foil			

Earth is made up of three types of rock: igneous, metamorphic, and sedimentary.

Read the descriptions of the three types of rock, then draw a line to match them with the picture of the correct rock.

Igneous rocks are created when hot, liquid rock rises from deep below the Earth's surface, cools and hardens. When the rock cools slowly, crystals form, giving some igneous rocks a grainy appearance.

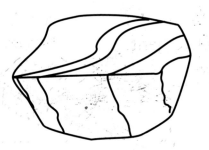

Marble

Sedimentary rocks form when layers of mud, sand, and other material settle on top of one another. Over thousands of years, they are pressed into solid rock.

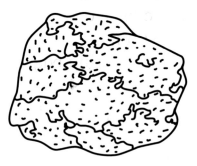

Granite

Metamorphic rocks form when solid rock is changed by extreme pressure and heat, often from volcanoes. They are very hard, smooth, and often have distinctive wavy or stripy patterns.

Sandstone

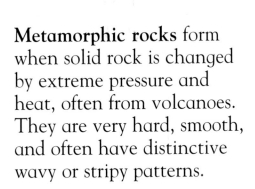

Rocks are everywhere. Mountains, hills, cliffs, stones, and pebbles are made of rock. Jewels are also made of rock. Garden soil and sand are made up of tiny bits of rock. Start your own collection.

TEST   **What You Need:**

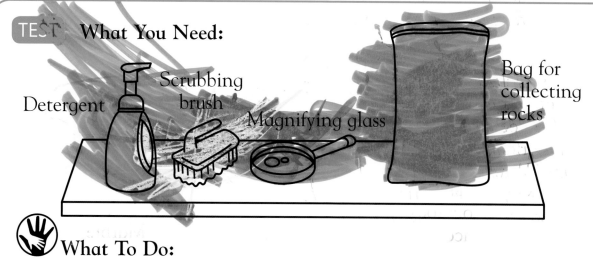

Detergent

Scrubbing brush

Magnifying glass

Bag for collecting rocks

What To Do:

1. Go with an adult to the park, the beach, or the backyard and look for rocks together. See how many rocks of different types and colors you can find. Check with an adult before you take any home in your collecting bag.

2. At home, wash the rocks in warm soapy water and scrub off any loose dirt. Leave the rocks to dry.

RESULT

Inspect each rock with the magnifying glass and fill in the table below. The colors often look brighter if you put the rock in water. Describe the rock. Notice the grains and see if the rock is spotted or striped.

	Rock 1	**Rock 2**	**Rock 3**
Where found?			
Color			
Hard or crumbly?			
Description			

A pond is a small body of fresh water.

Use the words in the box to name the animals in the pond, than color them in.

| Beaver | Dragonfly | Duck | Fish | Frog | Turtle |

A grassland is a habitat where most of the plants are grasses.
In North America, grasslands are called prairies.

Circle the animals that live in a grassland habitat.

| Bison | Hawk | Horse | Prairie dog | Wolf |

Certificate

Congratulations to

....

for successfully

finishing this book.

GOOD JOB!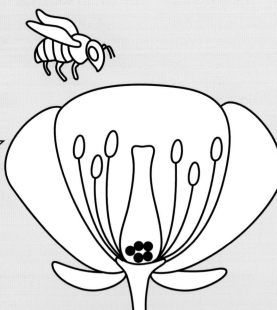

You're a star.

☆ ☆ ☆ ☆ ☆

Date

....

Answer Section
with Parents' Notes

This book is intended to support the science concepts that are taught in second grade.

Contents

Working through this book, your child will gain knowledge about:

- flowers and pollination;
- coniferous plants;
- insects;
- arachnids;
- animal life cycles;
- adaptation;
- endangered species;
- the digestive system;
- the respiratory system;
- the nervous system;
- friction;
- simple machines;
- chemical change;
- solutions;
- sound;
- water;
- evaporation and condensation;
- clouds;
- weather;
- air temperature;
- the seasons;
- rocks and minerals;
- habitats.

How to Help Your Child

This is the fourth in a series of DK Workbooks focused on science. The previous three were prepared for children in Pre-Kindergarten, Kindergarten, and first grade. The content in each book is aligned with the standard curriculum for that educational level. The books include various types of written activities to test your child's knowledge of earth science, life science, and physical science concepts. They also contain hands-on activities that can be assembled from simple, safe-to-use household items.

The hands-on activities are designed not just to test your child's knowledge, but also to give him or her practice in the basic skills of scientific investigation—following a plan, making observations and predictions, recording data, and drawing inferences and conclusions. Your child will need guidance from you when assembling the materials and reading the directions for many of the activities. The notes at the end of the book will assist you in doing that. The notes also contain additional information on many of the topics, ideas for more hands-on activities, as well as critical thinking questions that can help make this book an enjoyable and educational experience.

★ Scientists

FACTS

Scientists study different parts of Earth and nature.

Label the name of each scientist to complete the sentences.

| Botanist | Chemist | Zoologist |

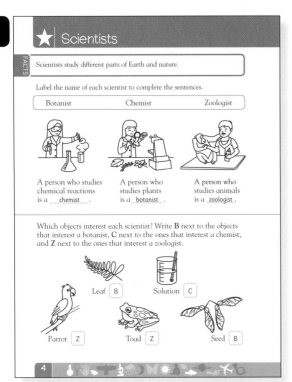

A person who studies chemical reactions is a __chemist__ .

A person who studies plants is a __botanist__ .

A person who studies animals is a __zoologist__ .

Which objects interest each scientist? Write **B** next to the objects that interest a botanist, **C** next to the ones that interest a chemist, and **Z** next to the ones that interest a zoologist.

Leaf [B] Solution [C]

Parrot [Z] Toad [Z] Seed [B]

Continue the discussion of scientists by asking your child if he or she would like to be a scientist one day. Ask "If you could be a scientist, what would you study? Why?" Discuss different types of scientific careers: medicine, botany, lab work, field study, chemicals, animals, physical sciences, etc.

Flowers ★

FACTS

Flowers contain the male and female parts of a plant. The male cells are a powder called pollen, and are produced in the stamen. Visiting animals, attracted by the colorful petals and scent of the flower, pick up the pollen from one flower and deposit it on another. The female part of a flower is called the pistil. When the pistil is dusted by the pollen of another flower, it is called pollination. When pollen moves down the pistil, seeds form. The seeds grow into new plants.

Use the words in the box to complete the sentences.

| Petals | Pistil | Pollen | Seed | Stamen |

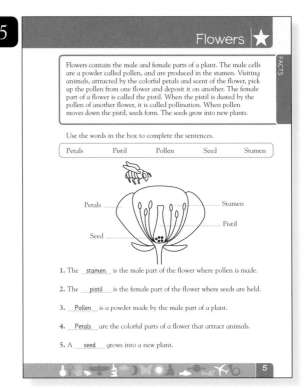

Petals

Seed

Stamen

Pistil

1. The __stamen__ is the male part of the flower where pollen is made.

2. The __pistil__ is the female part of the flower where seeds are held.

3. __Pollen__ is a powder made by the male part of a plant.

4. __Petals__ are the colorful parts of a flower that attract animals.

5. A __seed__ grows into a new plant.

Discuss the ways flowers attract pollinating insects and animals. Colorful petals are one way to attract pollinators. Sweet nectar is another. Another is the flower's scent. Discuss how different flowers have different scents, and ask why that might be.

★ Pollination

FACTS

Pollination is the transfer of pollen from one plant to another. Many flowering plants depend on honeybees to pollinate them.

These pictures show the steps a honeybee takes to pollinate a flower. Match each step with the sentence that describes what is happening in the picture.

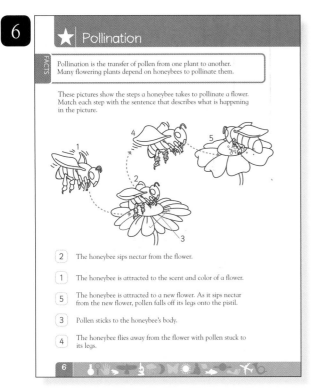

[2] The honeybee sips nectar from the flower.

[1] The honeybee is attracted to the scent and color of a flower.

[5] The honeybee is attracted to a new flower. As it sips nectar from the new flower, pollen falls off its legs onto the pistil.

[3] Pollen sticks to the honeybee's body.

[4] The honeybee flies away from the flower with pollen stuck to its legs.

Female and male animals mate to produce offspring. Something similar occurs in the plant world. A plant has a male part that makes pollen. That pollen is carried to the female part of the same plant or, more likely, to the female part of another plant of the same species. Fertilization takes place and a seed forms.

Pollinators ★

FACTS

Flowering plants depend on wind, water, and animals to pollinate them. Many different types of animals pass pollen from flower to flower as they feed.

Draw a line between the animal and the sentence that describes how it pollinates flowers.

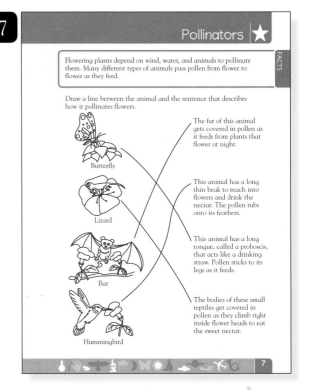

Butterfly

Lizard

Bat

Hummingbird

The fur of this animal gets covered in pollen as it feeds from plants that flower at night.

This animal has a long thin beak to reach into flowers and drink the nectar. The pollen rubs onto its feathers.

This animal has a long tongue, called a proboscis, that acts like a drinking straw. Pollen sticks to its legs as it feeds.

The bodies of these small reptiles get covered in pollen as they climb right inside flower heads to eat the sweet nectar.

Tell your child how pollination also helps the bees who carry the pollen from flower to flower: When honeybees return to their hive, the pollen left on their bodies comes into the hive as well. The worker bees mix the pollen with enzymes and microbes. The result is bee pollen or bee bread, a protein-rich concoction that the bees eat.

★ Conifers

FACTS

A conifer is a tree that produces its seeds in cones. Most coniferous trees are evergreen—they keep their leaves all year long. Some also have long, thin leaves called needles.

Circle the tree branches that belong to conifers.

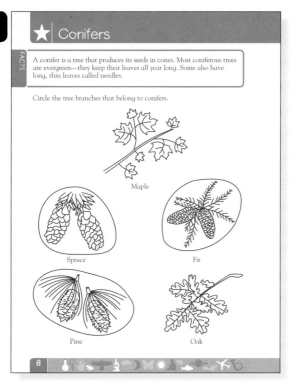

Maple

Spruce

Fir

Pine

Oak

Take a field trip with your child through your neighborhood, a local park, or a nearby forest. Identify which trees are coniferous. Look for needles and cones. Note the similarities and differences between the conifers: what do the needles and cones look like? Are they large or small? Do they have a distinct smell?

Carnivorous Plants ★

FACTS

Some plants are carnivorous. They trap and eat small animals, mostly insects.

Look at these three pictures of carnivorous plants, then read the descriptions below and complete the sentences.

Venus flytrap   Pitcher plant   Sundew

1. A _____sundew_____ has tentacles covered with a sweet, sticky goo. Insects attracted to the plant get stuck in the goo and are eaten.

2. A _____pitcher plant_____ has a deep cup full of a sweet nectar that lures insects into it. Hairs inside the cup keep the insects from getting out.

3. A _____venus flytrap_____ has leaves at the end of each stalk that open like a clamshell. When an insect lands on the leaves to drink the nectar, the leaves snap shut and trap the insect inside.

Why might a plant be carnivorous, rather than use sunlight for food? (Answer: Carnivorous plants grow in soils that lack certain nutrients that plants need to survive. To compensate, the plants derive those nutrients from the animals they trap and consume.)

★ Insects

FACTS

All insects have a body divided into three parts: the head, the thorax, where the legs and wings are attached, and the abdomen, which holds most of the animal's organs. Insects have six legs.

An ant is a common insect. Use the words in the box to label the parts of the ant.

| Abdomen | Antenna | Head | Leg | Thorax |

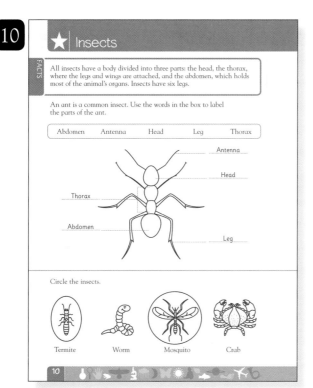

Antenna

Head

Thorax

Abdomen

Leg

Circle the insects.

Termite   Worm   Mosquito   Crab

Take a field trip with your child to a neighborhood park. Bring along a magnifying glass and an identification manual. Look for insects and identify which species they belong to. How many different types can you see? Remember not to disturb the insects; simply observe.

Social Insects ★

FACTS

Insects that live in a group are called social insects. Honeybees live together in a hive. Each type of bee has a special job. The queen bee lays all the eggs. The worker bees are females who gather food to feed the young bees. Drones are male bees who mate with the queen.

Use the words in the box to complete the crossword.

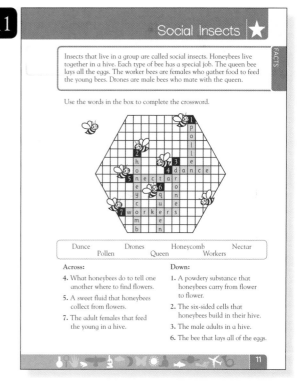

| Dance | | Drones | | Honeycomb | | Nectar |
| | Pollen | | Queen | | Workers | |

Across:
4. What honeybees do to tell one another where to find flowers.
5. A sweet fluid that honeybees collect from flowers.
7. The adult females that feed the young in a hive.

Down:
1. A powdery substance that honeybees carry from flower to flower.
2. The six-sided cells that honeybees build in their hive.
3. The male adults in a hive.
6. The bee that lays all of the eggs.

Honeybees aren't the only social animals. Name some other animals that live in groups. (Possible answers: chimpanzees, elephants, ants, termites, humans, wolves, bats, dolphins, hyenas.) Why might animals live in groups? (Possible answers: safety in numbers, shared care of offspring, help with finding food.)

★ Types of Insect

FACTS Scientists have found more than 900,000 types of insect.

Use the words in the box to name the insects.

Beetle	Cockroach	Dragonfly	Flea	Fly
Grasshopper		Ladybug		Wasp

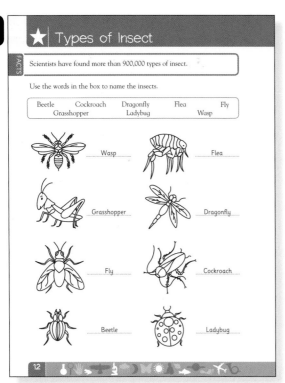

Wasp

Flea

Grasshopper

Dragonfly

Fly

Cockroach

Beetle

Ladybug

Ask your child: "What types of insect do you see on an average day?" Have your child list them (mosquitoes, gnats, ants, bees, dragonflies, beetles, etc.), and comment on their most recognizable characteristics. Are those insects beautiful? Interesting? Common? Rare?

Arachnids ★

FACTS Arachnids are animals that have two main body parts, and four pairs of legs. Arachnids include spiders, scorpions, ticks, and mites.

Study these pictures of four arachnids. Complete the chart that describes the ways in which arachnids look different from insects.

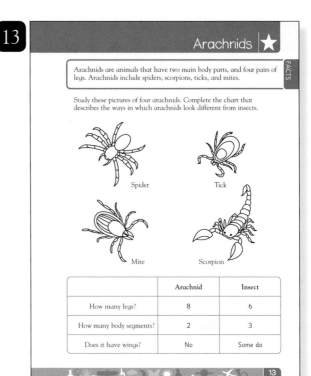

Spider

Tick

Mite

Scorpion

	Arachnid	Insect
How many legs?	8	6
How many body segments?	2	3
Does it have wings?	No	Some do

One of the best-known spiders is the daddy longlegs. The problem is, the daddy longlegs isn't a spider. It is a harvestmen, from a diffrent group of arachnid. Like spiders, harvestmen have eight legs. Unlike spiders, harvestmen have only one body segment, don't spin webs, and don't have venom. Spiders are carnivores, harvestmen are omnivores.

★ Life Cycle of a Butterfly

FACTS A butterfly is an insect that looks very different at each stage of its life. This change is called metamorphosis.

Use the words in the box to label each stage in the life of a butterfly and complete the sentences below.

Adult	Caterpillar	Chrysalis	Egg

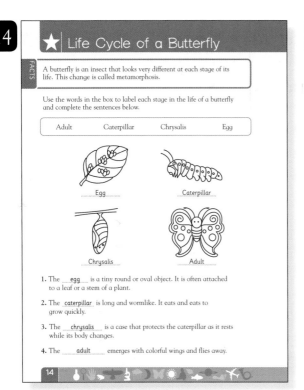

Egg

Caterpillar

Chrysalis

Adult

1. The ___egg___ is a tiny round or oval object. It is often attached to a leaf or a stem of a plant.

2. The ___caterpillar___ is long and wormlike. It eats and eats to grow quickly.

3. The ___chrysalis___ is a case that protects the caterpillar as it rests while its body changes.

4. The ___adult___ emerges with colorful wings and flies away.

Many people mistakenly call a chrysalis a "cocoon." A cocoon is a protective coat of silk spun by some types of moth for their metamorphosis. It is different from a butterfly's chrysalis. Butterflies do not make cocoons.

Life Cycle of a Grasshopper ★

FACTS A grasshopper is an example of an insect that has the same body shape throughout most of its life.

Use the words to label each stage in the life of a grasshopper and complete the sentences below.

Adult	Nymph	Egg

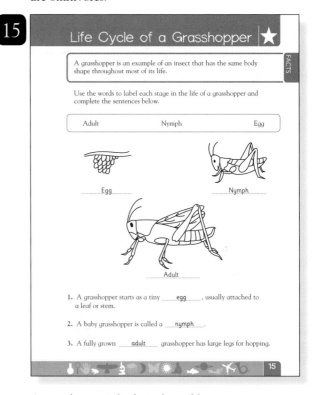

Egg

Nymph

Adult

1. A grasshopper starts as a tiny ___egg___, usually attached to a leaf or stem.

2. A baby grasshopper is called a ___nymph___.

3. A fully grown ___adult___ grasshopper has large legs for hopping.

A grasshopper's body is shaped by a strong external skeleton called an exoskeleton. As the insect grows, it sheds its old exoskeleton and a new one forms. This is called molting, and it happens many times over the life of the insect. Other animals molt, shedding whatever outer covering they have. Birds and dogs molt.

★ Life Cycle of a Frog

FACTS

A frog is an amphibian—it spends part of its life in water, and part on land. Frogs are very different at each stage of their life cycle. This change is called metamorphosis.

Use the words to label the stages in the life of a frog.

| Eggs | Frog | Froglet | Tadpole | Tadpole with legs |

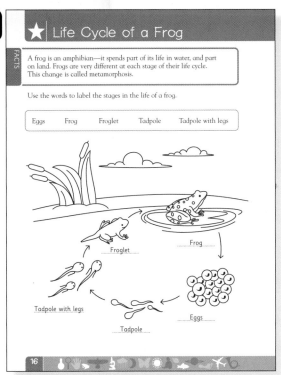

Froglet
Frog
Tadpole with legs
Eggs
Tadpole

In what way is the frog's life cycle more similar to the butterfly's life cycle than it is to the grasshopper's. (Answer: Both the frog and butterfly undergo changes in the shape of their bodies. The grasshopper looks much the same throughout its life cycle.)

Growth and Change ★

FACTS

All animals change as they mature into adulthood.

Draw lines between the young animals and the adult animals they will become.

Young Animals | Adult Animals

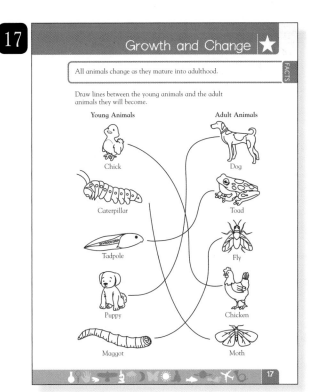

Chick
Caterpillar
Tadpole
Puppy
Maggot

Dog
Toad
Fly
Chicken
Moth

Discuss with your child how the human body changes as it develops from infancy to adulthood. Look at photos of when your child was an infant, a toddler, and now. Discuss the differences in size, proportion, shape, and development. For example, over time your child's fingers got longer and thinner, making it easier to hold a pencil.

★ Traits

FACTS

A trait is a distinguishing characteristic—the way something looks or behaves. Scientists study traits to understand how living things are related.

Write your name at the top of the second column and the names of two members of your family at the top of the other columns. Record the age, height, and other traits about you and your family members.

Traits	Relative	Your Name	Relative
Age			
Male or Female			
Height			
Eye color			
Hair color			
Shoe size			

Answers may vary

Compare the information.

What traits do you share with your relatives?
Answers may vary

What traits are different?
Answers may vary

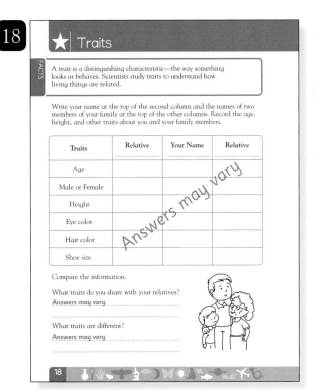

Have your child repeat this activity with friends. Compare the results. Are friends more or less like your child than family members are?

Adaptations ★

FACTS

An adaptation is a feature that helps living things to survive in the habitat they live in.

Read the sentences and match them to the correct animal by putting the number in the box. We have done the first one for you.

1. This animal's keen sense of hearing helps it detect prey at night.
2. This strong animal catches its prey with its sharp claws and strong jaws.
3. This animal uses its long tail to help it climb trees and cling to branches.
4. This animal has teeth strong enough to cut down trees to build dams.
5. This animal has a beak with a pouch so it can scoop up fish from the water.
6. This animal has a long neck so it can eat leaves high up in the trees.

4
5
6
2
3
1

Behaviors are adaptations, too. For example, some animals are nocturnal—they are active during the night. Why might they adapt to that kind of behavior? (Possible answers: To hide from predators. To avoid the heat of the day and conserve water, especially in deserts.)

★ Endangered Species

An endangered species is a plant or an animal that is in danger of becoming extinct, or dying out forever.

Use the words to name the endangered animals pictured below.

African wild dog   Chimpanzee   Giant Panda   Orangutan
Rhinoceros   Tiger

Rhinoceros

Tiger

Giant Panda

African Wild Dog

Chimpanzee

Orangutan

Discuss what might cause an animal to become endangered. What is going on in the world today that might harm some animals? Discuss the impact of human civilization on the animal kingdom. (Possible discussion points: pollution, climate change, overhunting, overfishing, and habitat destruction.)

Digestive System ★

The digestive system turns food into nutrients that our bodies need to survive.

Use the words in the box to complete the sentences.

Esophagus   Large Intestine   Mouth   Small Intestine   Stomach

Mouth

Esophagus

Stomach

Small intestine

Large intestine

1. The digestion process begins in the __mouth__, where food is chewed and mixed with saliva.
2. The __esophagus__ connects the mouth to the stomach.
3. The __stomach__ contains an acid fluid that breaks down food.
4. The __small intestine__ is a long tube where nutrients from digested food pass into the bloodstream.
5. The __large intestine__ mixes water with food that you can't digest and turns it into waste.

The small intestine can grow to more than 20 ft long, and folds over many times so it will fit in the human body. As food makes the long journey through the intestines, nutrients are absorbed through the intestine walls. That long trip allows the body to absorb the most nutrition possible from the food we eat.

★ Respiratory System

The cells of the body are supplied with the oxygen they need by the respiratory system. Air containing oxygen is breathed into the body and enters the bloodstream through the lungs. Carbon dioxide is breathed out as waste.

Use the words to label the parts of the respiratory system and to complete the sentences.

Lungs   Nose   Trachea

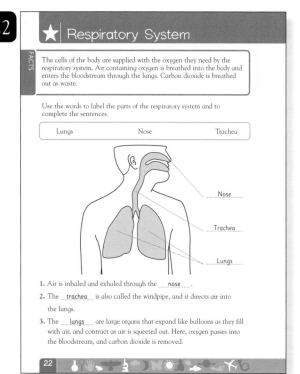

Nose

Trachea

Lungs

1. Air is inhaled and exhaled through the __nose__.
2. The __trachea__ is also called the windpipe, and it directs air into the lungs.
3. The __lungs__ are large organs that expand like balloons as they fill with air, and contract as air is squeezed out. Here, oxygen passes into the bloodstream, and carbon dioxide is removed.

This experiment shows how the diaphragm works. Cut the bottom off a soda bottle. Cover the bottom with a piece of plastic, securing with a rubber band. Insert a balloon into the bottle and stretch the opening over the bottle's mouth. Pull the plastic down, then push it up. The plastic acts like a diaphragm, and the balloon acts like the lungs.

Nervous System ★

The nervous system is made up of the brain, the spinal cord, and nerves. The brain controls the body by sending signals down the spinal cord. The spinal cord sends the signals back and forth between the brain and nerves all over the body.

Use the words to label the picture and to complete the sentences that explain the parts of the nervous system.

Brain   Spinal cord   Nerves

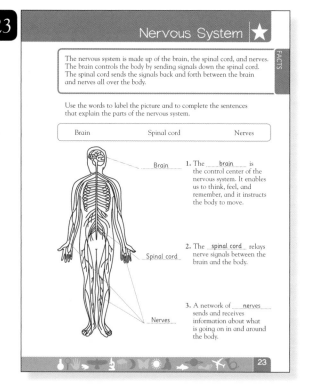

Brain

Spinal cord

Nerves

1. The __brain__ is the control center of the nervous system. It enables us to think, feel, and remember, and it instructs the body to move.

2. The __spinal cord__ relays nerve signals between the brain and the body.

3. A network of __nerves__ sends and receives information about what is going on in and around the body.

Ask your child if he or she has ever bumped their elbow and felt a tingling sensation shoot down their arm. That's your funny bone. It isn't really a bone; it's part of a nerve. At the elbow, the nerve passes close to the skin. When you bump your elbow, you hit the nerve. That same nerve runs through the humerus bone in your upper arm.

★ Friction

FACTS

The resistance that occurs where surfaces rub together is a force called friction. Rough surfaces create more friction. Smooth surfaces create less friction.

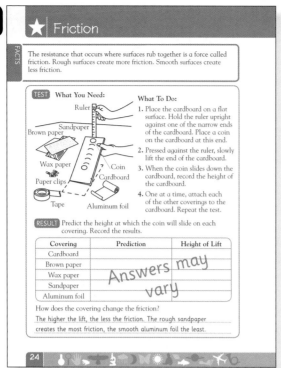

TEST What You Need:

Ruler
Sandpaper
Brown paper
Wax paper
Coin
Paper clips
Cardboard
Tape
Aluminum foil

What To Do:

1. Place the cardboard on a flat surface. Hold the ruler upright against one of the narrow ends of the cardboard. Place a coin on the cardboard at this end.
2. Pressed against the ruler, slowly lift the end of the cardboard.
3. When the coin slides down the cardboard, record the height of the cardboard.
4. One at a time, attach each of the other coverings to the cardboard. Repeat the test.

RESULT Predict the height at which the coin will slide on each covering. Record the results.

Covering	Prediction	Height of Lift
Cardboard		
Brown paper		
Wax paper	*Answers may*	
Sandpaper	*vary*	
Aluminum foil		

How does the covering change the friction?
The higher the lift, the less the friction. The rough sandpaper creates the most friction, the smooth aluminum foil the least.

Try this cool activity. Using two phone books, interlace the pages of one book over the pages of other (like shuffling a deck of cards) until all of them overlap and the two books hold together. Try pulling them apart. Try again. You can't, because friction between the pages holds the books together.

Friction and Sports ★

FACTS

Friction helps people play sports. In some sports, you need high friction to help grip smooth surfaces. In other sports, you need low friction so that things slide over surfaces smoothly.

The arrows point to places where friction is important in each sport. Check (✔) whether there is high friction or low friction at this point. Then explain how that amount of friction helps people play each sport.

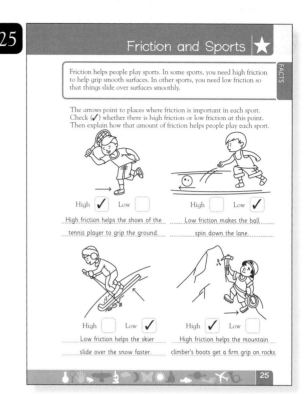

High [✔] Low [ ]
High friction helps the shoes of the tennis player to grip the ground.

High [ ] Low [✔]
Low friction makes the ball spin down the lane.

High [ ] Low [✔]
Low friction helps the skier slide over the snow faster.

High [✔] Low [ ]
High friction helps the mountain climber's boots get a firm grip on rocks.

Discuss with your child how friction might play a role in the sports he or she likes to play. Imagine if the friction they need (between their sneakers and the basketball court) weren't there. Would they still be able to play basketball? What would happen if something with low friction (a body swimming through water, for instance) suddenly had high friction?

★ Simple Machines

FACTS

Simple machines make work easier for us. They allow us to push or pull things over greater distances.

Use the words in the box to complete the definitions of six simple machines, then draw a line between each sentence and the machine it describes.

| Inclined plane | Lever | Pulley | Screw | Wedge | Wheel |

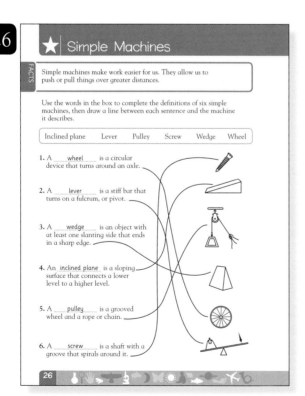

1. A _wheel_ is a circular device that turns around an axle.

2. A _lever_ is a stiff bar that turns on a fulcrum, or pivot.

3. A _wedge_ is an object with at least one slanting side that ends in a sharp edge.

4. An _inclined plane_ is a sloping surface that connects a lower level to a higher level.

5. A _pulley_ is a grooved wheel and a rope or chain.

6. A _screw_ is a shaft with a groove that spirals around it.

We use or depend on many tools and machines throughout the day. (Examples: cars, bicycles, screwdrivers, DVD players, dishwashers.) Which parts of each one are simple machines?

Simple Machines in Action ★

FACTS

Simple machines can help us do many jobs.

Circle the six simple machines that are being used in this picture.

Try this activity with your child to demonstrate how wheels make it easier to do work. Put a very heavy book on a table and push it across the table. Now place several plastic straws, spaced several inches apart from one another, under the book. Push again. Which push was easier?

★ Levers

The point at which a lever turns is called a fulcrum. The fulcrum needs to be in the right place for the lever to work properly.

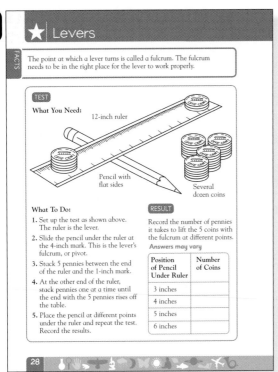

TEST

What You Need:
12-inch ruler

Pencil with flat sides

Several dozen coins

What To Do:

1. Set up the test as shown above. The ruler is the lever.
2. Slide the pencil under the ruler at the 4-inch mark. This is the lever's fulcrum, or pivot.
3. Stack 5 pennies between the end of the ruler and the 1-inch mark.
4. At the other end of the ruler, stack pennies one at a time until the end with the 5 pennies rises off the table.
5. Place the pencil at different points under the ruler and repeat the test. Record the results.

RESULT

Record the number of pennies it takes to lift the 5 coins with the fulcrum at different points.

Answers may vary

Position of Pencil Under Ruler	Number of Coins
3 inches	
4 inches	
5 inches	
6 inches	

Levers come in many forms. Have your child use these levers and identify where the fulcrum is in each one: Play on a seesaw. Cut paper with a pair of scissors. Use a hammer to pull a nail out of a board. Use a bottle opener to remove the cap from a bottle.

Matter ★

Matter is the name used to describe all the different material that makes up the universe. The amount of matter in an object is known as its mass. Matter also takes up space, which is known as its volume. There are three states of matter: solid, liquid, and gas. A solid keeps its shape. A liquid flows, and takes the shape of the container it is in. A gas expands to fill its container.

Use the words in the box to complete the sentences about matter.

Gas	Liquid	Mass	Solid	States	Volume

The Three States of Matter

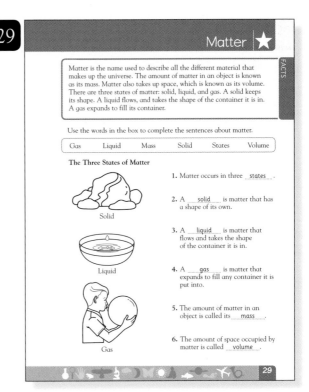

Solid

Liquid

Gas

1. Matter occurs in three __states__.

2. A __solid__ is matter that has a shape of its own.

3. A __liquid__ is matter that flows and takes the shape of the container it is in.

4. A __gas__ is matter that expands to fill any container it is put into.

5. The amount of matter in an object is called its __mass__.

6. The amount of space occupied by matter is called __volume__.

Solids, liquids, and gases are the three familiar phases of ordinary matter. There's also a fourth phase, called plasma. It's produced by very, very high temperatures, as in the sun and stars. Scientists estimate that the temperature at the core of the sun is about 27 million degrees Fahrenheit.

★ How Things Change

Some foods change when they get hot or cold.

Look at these questions about what happens to foods when the temperature changes. Put a check (✓) next to the correct answer.

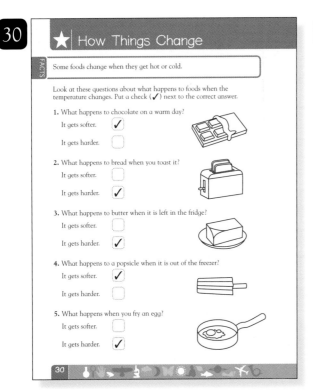

1. What happens to chocolate on a warm day?
   It gets softer. ✓
   It gets harder. ☐

2. What happens to bread when you toast it?
   It gets softer. ☐
   It gets harder. ✓

3. What happens to butter when it is left in the fridge?
   It gets softer. ☐
   It gets harder. ✓

4. What happens to a popsicle when it is out of the freezer?
   It gets softer. ✓
   It gets harder. ☐

5. What happens when you fry an egg?
   It gets softer. ☐
   It gets harder. ✓

A physical change is a change in the way matter looks and behaves. It does not produce a new substance. Water freezing, sugar dissolving in water, and a bottle breaking are physical changes. Cooking food also causes physical change. Discuss with your child the physical changes that happen to their favorite foods when you cook them.

Solutions ★

A solution is a mixture in which the different substances mix together so well that they seem like a single substance.

Put a check (✓) next to the substances that make a solution when added to water.

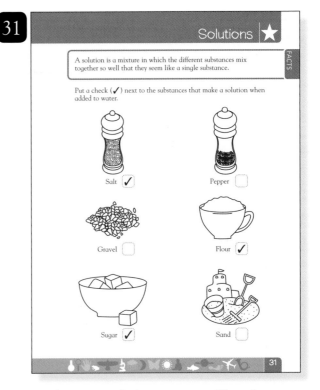

Salt ✓

Pepper ☐

Gravel ☐

Flour ✓

Sugar ✓

Sand ☐

A solution is made from two parts. The substance that dissolves is called the solute. The substance it dissolves in is called the solvent. Ask your child: "Which are the solutes and which are the solvents in this activity?"

★ Sound

Sounds can be made in many different ways.

Use the words in the box to describe correctly how these musical instruments are played to make sounds.

| Beating | Blowing | Plucking | Scraping | Shaking |

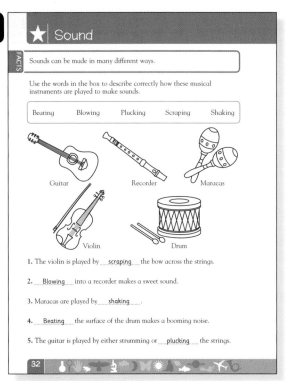

Guitar   Recorder   Maracas

Violin   Drum

1. The violin is played by __scraping__ the bow across the strings.

2. __Blowing__ into a recorder makes a sweet sound.

3. Maracas are played by __shaking__ .

4. __Beating__ the surface of the drum makes a booming noise.

5. The guitar is played by either strumming or __plucking__ the strings.

Sounds occur when an object vibrates, which causes the air around it to vibrate. The vibrations travel through the air. When they reach your eardrum, it vibrates, too, setting off a chain of movements in your inner ear and stimulating a nerve that relays a message to your brain.

Making Sounds ★

You can make a sound by blowing over the neck of a bottle. The sound will change if you pour water into the bottle.

TEST What You Need:

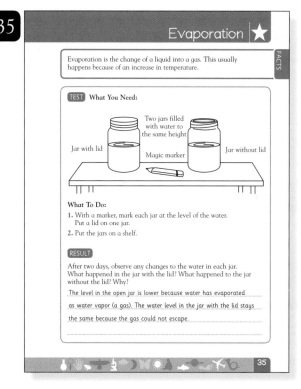

Water   Bottle with a narrow neck

What To Do:

1. Take the empty bottle, with the lid off, and place it on a table. Practice blowing over the neck until you can hear a hollow sound. Remember what the noise sounds like.

2. Pour some water into the bottle and blow again. Listen carefully to the sound again.

3. Add more water, a little at a time, and blow again. Note if the sound is changing.

RESULT

What happened to the sound when you added more and more water?

The pitch or the tone of the sound gets higher as you add more

water to the bottle.

The speed at which sound vibrates determines its pitch. When you blow across a bottleneck, the air vibrates inside the bottle, making a sound. When there is lots of room in the bottle, air vibrates slowly, producing a low sound. When you add water, the air has less space to move and vibrates faster, giving a higher sound.

★ Water

Water changes state when it freezes.

TEST What You Need:

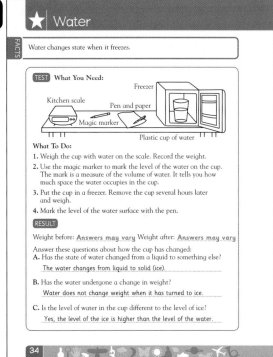

Freezer

Kitchen scale   Pen and paper

Magic marker

Plastic cup of water

What To Do:

1. Weigh the cup with water on the scale. Record the weight.

2. Use the magic marker to mark the level of the water on the cup. The mark is a measure of the volume of water. It tells you how much space the water occupies in the cup.

3. Put the cup in a freezer. Remove the cup several hours later and weigh.

4. Mark the level of the water surface with the pen.

RESULT

Weight before: __Answers may vary__ Weight after: __Answers may vary__

Answer these questions about how the cup has changed:

A. Has the state of water changed from a liquid to something else?

The water changes from liquid to solid (ice).

B. Has the water undergone a change in weight?

Water does not change weight when it has turned to ice.

C. Is the level of water in the cup different to the level of ice?

Yes, the level of the ice is higher than the level of the water.

Unlike most liquids, water expands when it freezes. This happens because the crystal structure of ice molecules contains more open space than liquid water molecules. But because the extra space in ice is taken up by air (which is weightless), ice weighs the same as liquid water.

Evaporation ★

Evaporation is the change of a liquid into a gas. This usually happens because of an increase in temperature.

TEST What You Need:

Two jars filled with water to the same height

Jar with lid   Magic marker   Jar without lid

What To Do:

1. With a marker, mark each jar at the level of the water. Put a lid on one jar.

2. Put the jars on a shelf.

RESULT

After two days, observe any changes to the water in each jar. What happened in the jar with the lid? What happened to the jar without the lid? Why?

The level in the open jar is lower because water has evaporated

as water vapor (a gas). The water level in the jar with the lid stays

the same because the gas could not escape.

Have your child repeat the activity, but this time fill several jars with different types of liquid—water, milk, juice, soda, and so on. Do they evaporate? If so, do they evaporate at the same rate as water? Which one evaporates fastest? Slowest? Make a chart of the results.

★ Condensation

FACTS

Condensation is the process in which a gas turns into liquid.
This usually happens because of a drop in temperature.

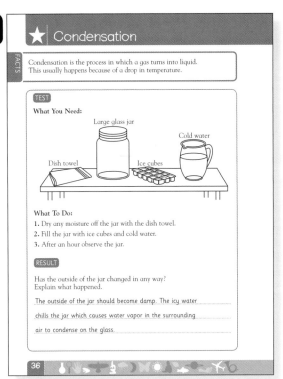

TEST

What You Need:

Large glass jar

Cold water

Dish towel   Ice cubes

What To Do:

1. Dry any moisture off the jar with the dish towel.
2. Fill the jar with ice cubes and cold water.
3. After an hour observe the jar.

RESULT

Has the outside of the jar changed in any way?
Explain what happened.

The outside of the jar should become damp. The icy water

chills the jar which causes water vapor in the surrounding

air to condense on the glass.

Have your child try this experiment. Have them
exhale on a window. What happens? Why?
(Answer: Human breath contains water vapor,
which condenses when it hits a cool windowpane,
causing a layer of water to form on the window.)

Water Cycle ★

FACTS

Water is constantly evaporating into the air, condensing as it
rises and cools, and falling back to Earth as rain. This movement
occurs in a circular pattern, called the water cycle.

Add arrows to this diagram to show the direction of the water cycle
and then complete the sentences below.

Clouds	Condenses	Evaporates	Water Cycle

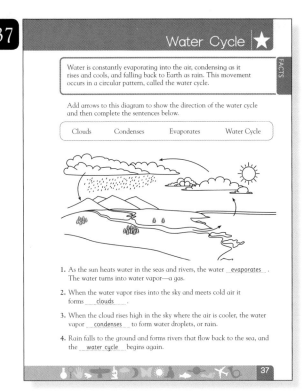

1. As the sun heats water in the seas and rivers, the water   evaporates .
   The water turns into water vapor—a gas.

2. When the water vapor rises into the sky and meets cold air it
   forms   clouds .

3. When the cloud rises high in the sky where the air is cooler, the water
   vapor   condenses   to form water droplets, or rain.

4. Rain falls to the ground and forms rivers that flow back to the sea, and
   the   water cycle   begins again.

The water cycle happens all around us. With your
child, identify the bodies of water in your area—
puddles, ponds, lakes, streams, reservoirs, etc.
Where does their water come from? Where does it
go? How does rainfall in the area find its way to
the ocean? Which mountains, rivers, streams take
it there?

★ Measuring Rainfall

FACTS

You can measure the amount of rain that falls over
a period of time in a rain gauge.

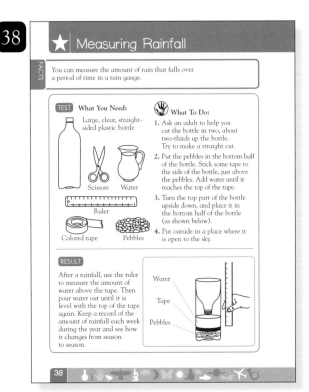

TEST **What You Need:**

Large, clear, straight-
sided plastic bottle

Scissors   Water

Ruler

Colored tape   Pebbles

✋ **What To Do:**

1. Ask an adult to help you
   cut the bottle in two, about
   two-thirds up the bottle.
   Try to make a straight cut.

2. Put the pebbles in the bottom half
   of the bottle. Stick some tape to
   the side of the bottle, just above
   the pebbles. Add water until it
   reaches the top of the tape.

3. Turn the top part of the bottle
   upside down, and place it in
   the bottom half of the bottle
   (as shown below).

4. Put outside in a place where it
   is open to the sky.

RESULT

After a rainfall, use the ruler
to measure the amount of
water above the tape. Then
pour water out until it is
level with the top of the tape
again. Keep a record of the
amount of rainfall each week
during the year and see how
it changes from season
to season.

Water

Tape

Pebbles

Rainfall is critical to all ecosystems. Discuss with
your child the ecosystem in which you live and
how rainfall impacts it. Are there lots of trees and
plants in your area that need rain? Do you live in
a desert community that receives little rainfall?
How does too little or too much rain impact
plants, animals, and people?

Weather ★

FACTS

Weather changes from day to day.

Record the weather conditions each day for a week in the chart below.
The words in the box below may help you.

Calm	Cloudy	Rainy	Snowy	Sunny	Windy

Day	Weather
Monday	
Tuesday	
Wednesday	
Thursday	
Friday	
Saturday	
Sunday	

Answers may vary

Repeat the activity. This time have your child
read or watch a weather report each evening
and record the next day's forecast. Compare it to
his or her next-day observations. How accurate
was the forecast?